MW01609377

First edition 2025

ISBN 978-1-7779609-3-3

This book was typeset in Burger Doodle Two NF, Comic Sans MS, and Helvetica.
The illustrations were created via free-hand sketch,
then digitally tweaked by yours truly.

my roommate is the WORST!

A furry roommate goes from bad to best.

written and illustrated by
Heather Rae Beauchesne

Written & illustrated by
Heather Rae Beauchesne

Dedicated to Bri, Izzy, Ariel, Nori, Aidan & Rocky

Cooking is
not one of my
strengths, yet
she expects me
to make all of
her meals.

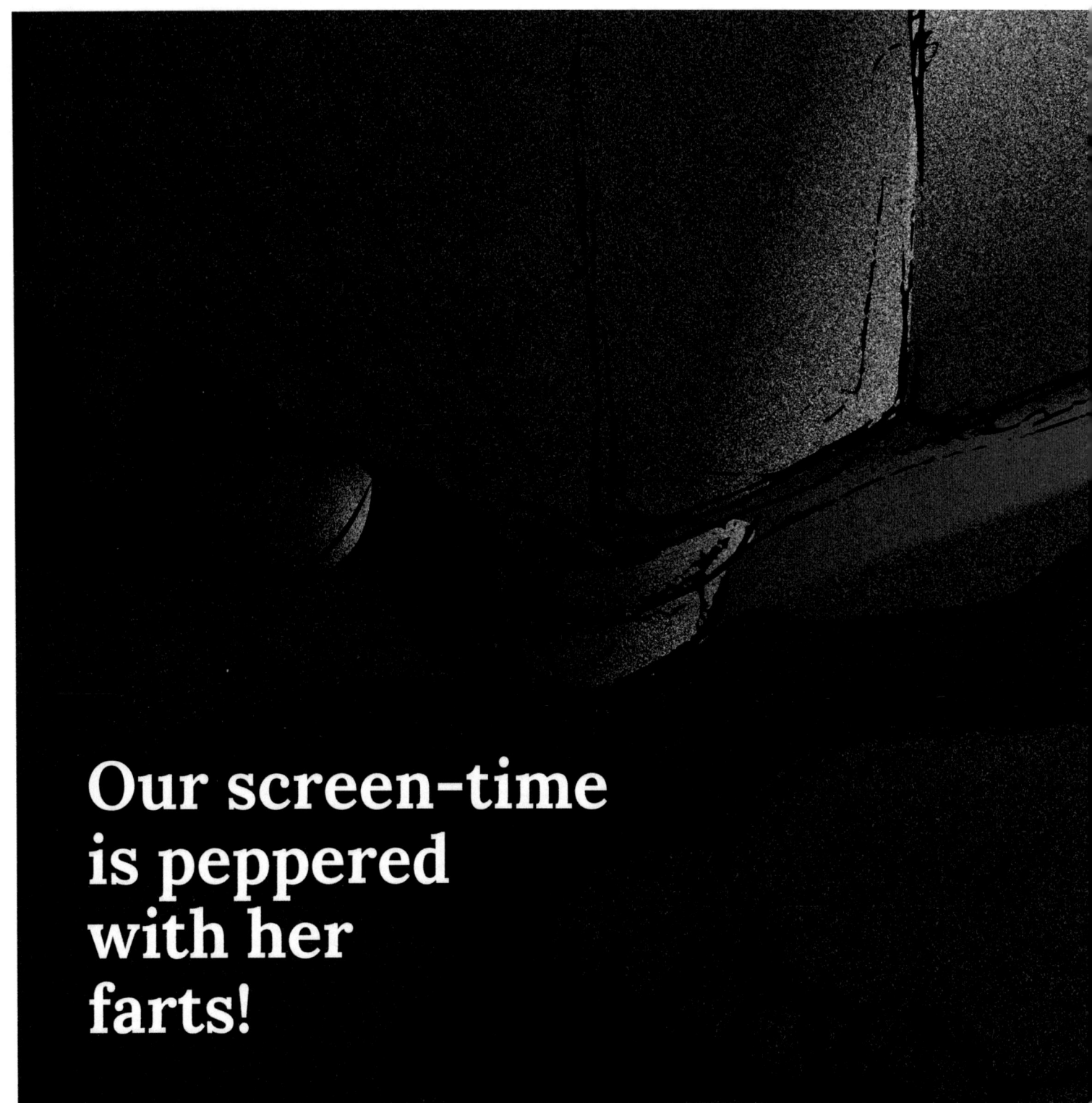

Our screen-time is peppered with her farts!

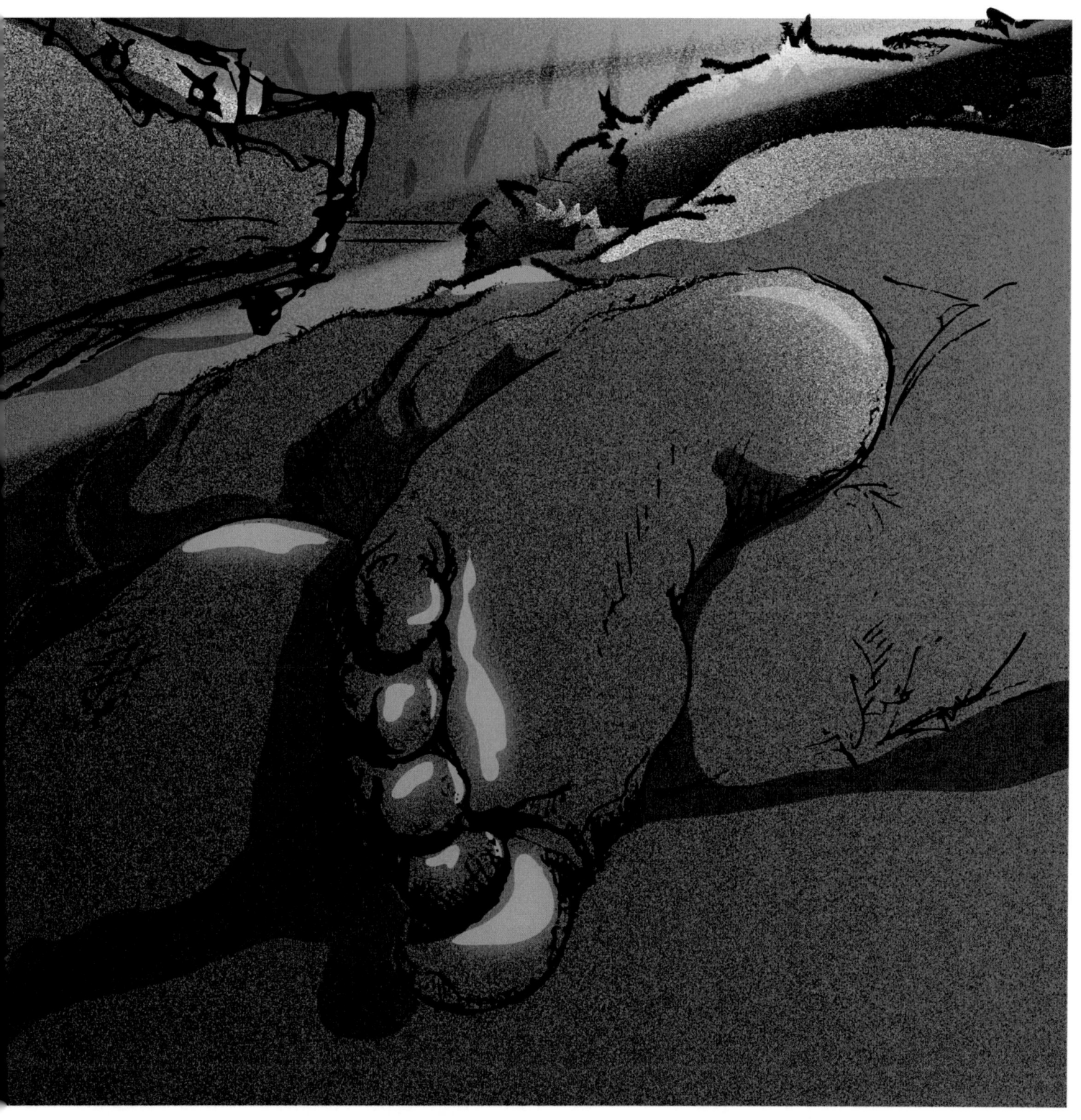

She never helps when there are chores to do. If you ask me, not my parents, she makes way more of a mess than I do.

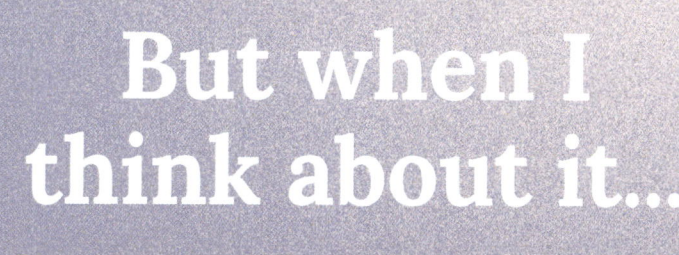

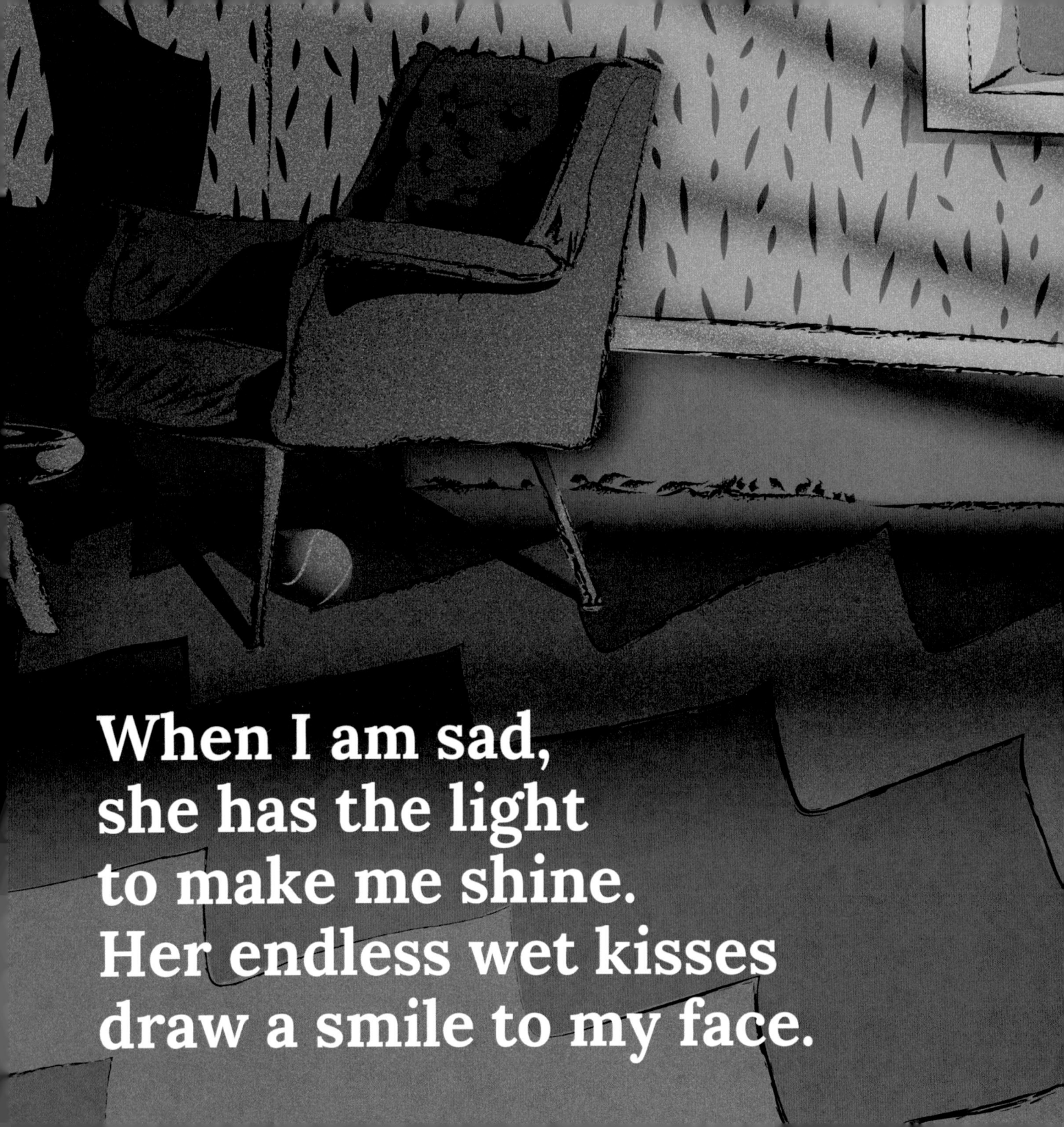

When I am sad,
she has the light
to make me shine.
Her endless wet kisses
draw a smile to my face.

When I am energenic, she is the first to suggest a walk. Sniffing out trails that lead to exciting ponds and muddy bogs is one of her more refined skills!

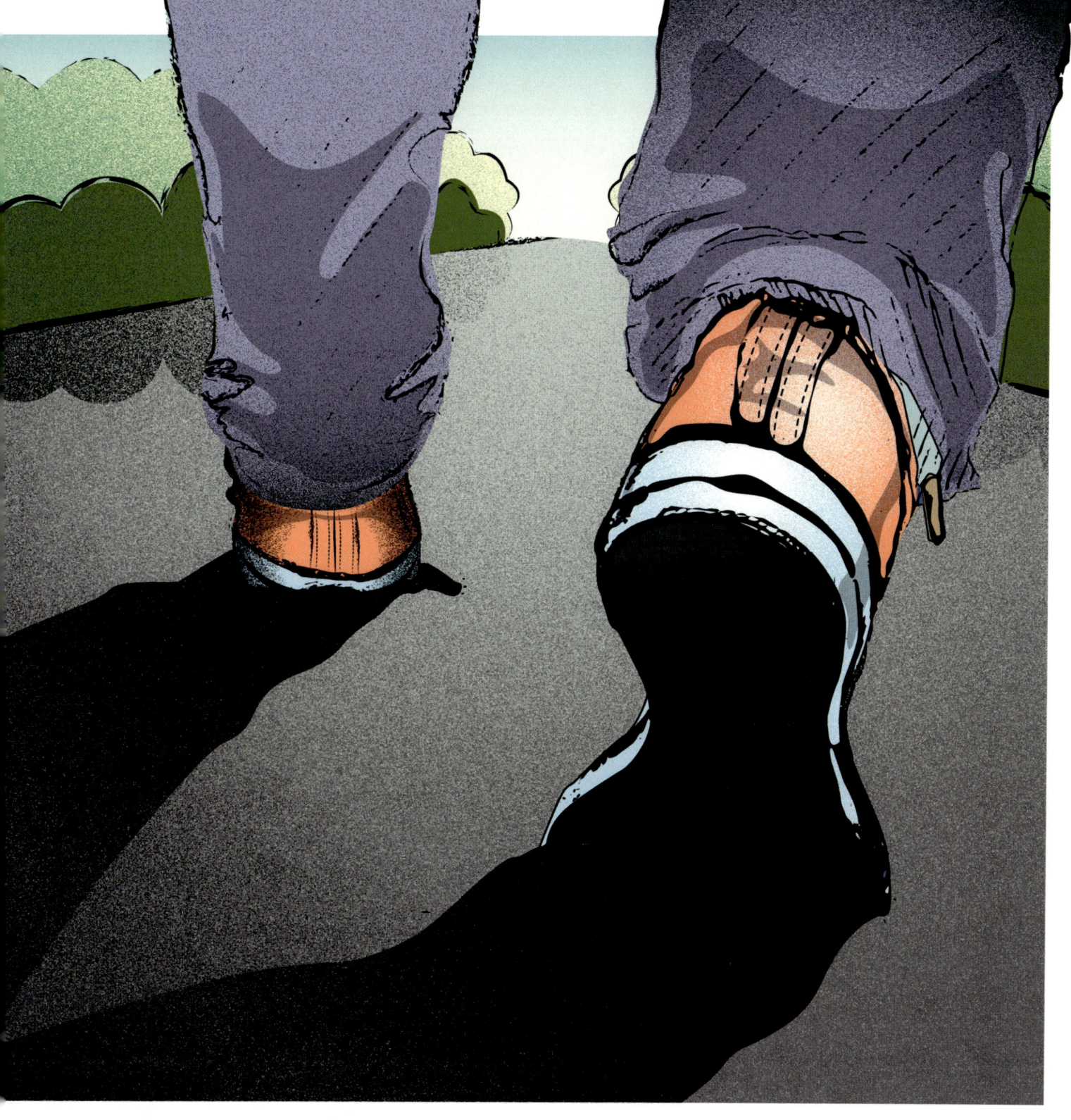

When I am calm,
she is right there chilling
beside me. Snacks are
shared lick-by-lick, bite-by-
bite. Rainbow popsicles are
our favorite!

When I am grumpy, she knows just how to lighten the mood.

Her wiggle n' bounce
performance
simply makes
me giddy!

When it is time
to get away, she is
more than happy to
come along. Beef jerky
promises will usually get
her out of the driver's seat!

And every day,
I am thankful to have
her by my side. No moment
is too chilly in the warmth
of our friendship.

About the author

Heather Rae Beauchesne is a studio artist; author-illustrator;
gallery curator; physical therapist; community
arts, culture, and health and wellbeing advocate;
and furry roommate enthusiast.

My Roommate is the Worst! is Beauchesne's
first children's book endeavor.

Manufactured by Amazon.ca
Bolton, ON

51171109R00024